It was raining. The children were fed up.
Biff and Anneena were bored, and Chip
was in a bad mood. He wanted to play
with the frisbee.

Mum had an idea. She had a new
jigsaw puzzle. She gave it to the children.
"You can do this jigsaw," she said. "It's
a good one."

Everyone looked at the jigsaw. It was a picture of soldiers and a boy.

"The soldiers are asking the boy a question," said Mum. "They want to know where his father is."

The jigsaw puzzle had lots of pieces. The children liked the jigsaw, but it was hard to do. Soon, Chip got bored with it. He began to play with the frisbee.

In the end, everyone got bored. The
magic key began to glow. The magic took
the children into a new adventure.

The magic took the children to a time long ago. It took them to a big house. Some children were playing with their mother and father.

Kipper looked at the children.
"What funny clothes they're wearing," he
said.

"They look like the children in the
picture on the jigsaw," said Anneena.

Kipper spoke to the girl and boy.
"Hello," he said "My name's Kipper.
This is Biff, Chip and Anneena."
"What funny names!" said the girl.
"And what funny clothes you're wearing."

"What are your names?" asked Chip.

"My name is Jane," said the girl.

"My name is Edmund," said the boy, "and my father is very important."

"We don't mind," said Kipper.

Edmund had never seen a frisbee before.
"Why have you got a plate?" he asked.
"It's not a plate," said Kipper. "It's a frisbee."
Everyone played with it.

Suddenly, there was a shout. A man ran towards Edmund's father.

"Quickly, you must hide!" he said. "Get inside the house. The soldiers are coming!"

Edmund's father ran inside.

"Quickly!" shouted Edmund. "We must help my father to hide. The soldiers mustn't find him."

Everyone ran into the house.

The soldiers came to the house. They knocked on the door.

"Let us in!" they shouted. "Open the door, or we'll smash it down."

Everyone ran to the library. The library
had a secret room. The room was behind a
bookcase. Edmund's father hid in the
secret room.

"Good luck, Father," said Edmund.

Edmund's mother pushed the bookcase back.

"Don't tell the soldiers about the secret room," said Jane. "They will kill my father if they find him."

The soldiers ran into the house. They looked for Edmund's father.

"Tell us where he is!" they shouted. The children were frightened, but they didn't say anything.

The soldiers looked everywhere, but they couldn't find Edmund's father. One of the soldiers found a sword.

"His sword is here," he said, "so he must be here somewhere."

The soldiers took everyone into a room.
Some men sat at a big table. They looked
at the children. One of them looked at
Kipper.

"Come here, little boy," he said.

"Where is your father?" asked the man.
Kipper was frightened, but he didn't say
anything. None of the children said
anything.

The important men were angry.

"Your father is hiding," they shouted. "Tell us where he is. If he is hiding in this house, we will soon find him."

Nobody said anything, so the soldiers
began to pull up the floor. They tapped on
the walls. Edmund's mother was
frightened.

"They may find him," she said.

Edmund and Jane were frightened. They wanted to help their father. Suddenly, Chip had an idea.

"Maybe your father could escape, if he dressed up as a woman," he said.

Biff and Anneena had an idea too. Biff
threw the frisbee at a soldier. The soldier
laughed. He had never seen a frisbee
before.

"Come and look at this!" he shouted.

The soldiers wanted a rest, so they stopped looking for Edmund's father. They all went outside and played with the frisbee. Soon, everyone was laughing.

The soldiers liked the frisbee. They
played with it for a long time. Suddenly,
an old woman came up. She looked very
poor. She wanted some money.

The soldiers stopped playing with the
frisbee. They shouted at the old woman.
"Go away!" they shouted. "We don't
have any money."

Suddenly, one of the soldiers looked at
the house. He saw someone running away.
"Look! Over there!" he shouted.
"Someone's running away."

The soldiers chased the woman.

"It's not a woman, it's a man," they
shouted. "It must be the man we want.
Don't let him get away."

The soldiers caught the man and took him back to the house.

"Oh no!" said Anneena. "They've caught Edmund's father. Our idea didn't work."

The soldiers thought they had caught
Edmund's father. But it was a trick.
"Grrr!" said the soldiers.
"Hooray!" said the children.

The children found some old clothes.
"So Edmund's father was the old
woman," said Anneena.
"What a good trick," laughed everyone.
Suddenly, the magic key began to glow.

The jigsaw puzzle was finished. Mum
looked at something in the picture.

"That's funny," she said. "That looks
like a frisbee."

"It must be a plate," said Chip.